Fallen Angels

Darnell Cabbagestalk

Fallen Angels

First Edition: 2023

ISBN: 9781524318666
ISBN eBook: 9781524328665

© of the text:
 Darnell Cabbagestalk

© Layout, design and production of this edition: 2023 EBL

All rights reserved. No part of this publication may be reproduced, distributed, or transmitted in any form or by any means, including photocopying, recording, or other electronic or mechanical methods, without the prior written permission of the Publisher.

*I would like to dedicate my book to the Boys:
Lee, Smith, Benton, and Dingle.
Without them, I would be normal.*

Table of Contents

Thank You/I'm Sorry 9
Ecstasy..11
New Day...13
Family 15
Kindness 17
Love 19
For My Daughter..21
Security..23
Men Hurt Too..25
Emotions 27
Her...29
Time Goes By...31
Would've, Could've, Should've... 33
Self Care...35
Moving on 37
Mental Breakdown..39
Letting Things Happen 41

Wild Side	43
Black Love	45
What I Like	47
Sabotage	49
Trust	51
Doubt	53

Thank You/I'm Sorry

The laughter, the teasing
Playful laughter and no deceiving
The late night talks
The long but blissful walks

You opening up and showing me who you are
You were there for even when shit got hard
You comforted me made me strong
Corrected me when I was wrong

The vibe was always amazing
We connected so fast it was crazy
But I couldn't out run my past
and myself look like an ass

Instead of trying to be in control
I should've gone with the flow
Then I pushed you away
And I regret to this day

Let's go back to when we were wild and free

Start over again waste time with me

No more trauma

No more drama

Fun free

Almost like we are in a fantasy

You always stood by my side

I got one extra ticket, wanna get back on this ride?

Ecstasy

Your curves, something so sensual

When I see you so many thoughts in my mental

Those eyes

Big and wide

Stops me in my tracks

Throws my hormones outta whack

The way you walk

The way you talk

Your movements so enticing

When you moan, that's what drives me

Your taste so sweet and divine

While running my hand down your thigh

Caressing you in my arms

Normally I'm gentle, but tonight I'm going hard

Every touch, every whisper

As I drive deeper and deeper

Uhh!

Ahhh!

In passion that can't be tamed
The love that we share is the same
And it shows when you call out my name
Your lips soft and moist
You never disappoint
And then I put my hands on your knees
And think of you as a book I want to read
The taste of you makes my mind race
So wet I'm about to hydrate

Then I flip you over and grab your waist
Then I drive with power and grace
I hear you shiver and moan
I go until I can't anymore

New Day

I went through what I had to go through
I got over what I needed to overcome
Old wounds start to sooth
My heart beats like a smooth drum
I leave the past in the past

Family

The ones that go the extra mile

As soon as you feel their presence you smile.

The ones that warm your heart

Your biggest supporters from the start.

An undeniable bond

A love that travels from this life into the beyond.

They are the ones that can cause insanity

They are your family.

Kindness

To find a sense of one's self,
You must learn to forgive someone else.
Hatred, anger, and rage
Is what we have to overcome in this day and age.

You hurt my feelings, I hurt yours;
Honestly it's meaningless actions and words.
Tell someone you love them. Tell 'em you care
Because one day they won't be there.

Tomorrow is never promised,
Yesterday has expired.
Look at yourself and be honest,
Don't let something temporary transpire.

Be gentle and understanding,
Uplift someone and they become family.
It's easier to love than it is to hate,
Your kindness will introduce you to something great.

Love

It can seem so healthy but hurt so much
A river that flows and is soothing to the touch
When you look at them a smile starts
Or when they talk you feel warm at heart

It takes no less than everything
But gives you so many memories
Even in the worst days you make me smile
And when you laugh it makes me feel wild

You look perfect in every way
Even when you're leaving, I want you to stay
And every time you make me you smile
I'll stop the world for you, if it gives us time

When you love someone, it's amazing
It's almost as if your heart's racing
You gave me something to lose
Because there's no one more precious than you

For My Daughter

Someone to protect you
When something goes wrong
You have someone to talk to
No matter the problem, no matter how long.

When you're scared and don't have a clue
When you're having a hard time even at two
To reassure you matters because, baby, you do.

When you get a little wild and a little mean
I'm the one to show you you're a queen
I know what that connection is
And how much it means, even as a kid.

To pick up the pieces of your broken heart
Someone to remind you that, girl, you're smart
Someone to teach you to care from the start.

Someone to teach you how to be sweet
To teach you how to be tough
To teach you to think on your feet
To show you you're more than enough
You'll never be alone in this world
Because darling you're my baby girl.

Security

Someone that you can be devoted too
You both put in effort and love comes soon
The trust, comfort, vulnerability is there
You melt in their eyes while they stare
Communication is at its highest peak
You're so in sync you don't have to speak
You can trust them in every facet
Because your heart is their most prized asset
The feelings and emotions are high intensity
Because between the two of you there is security

Men Hurt Too

Men ain't shit. Men are dogs.
Damn we've heard it all.
The good ones get hurt and left behind,
Then they turn bad and everyone ask why.

They preach about men opening up.
They try to teach us about trust.
When we become vulnerable
Is when the world makes us uncomfortable.

It starts young. "Stop crying. Be strong."
"Being hard is the only way you'll belong."

Then we grow into men full of toxicity
Then we get wives and becomes domesticity
Please, reading this don't get confused.
Ladies men hurt too.

Emotions

They come in waves; the rush, the thrill
Feelings that come are so addicting, it can kill
The feeling of happy makes you strong
Sadness comes, make you feel alone
Anger is like a fire that spreads in the night
Lust can lead you into situations that bite
The process of controlling these feelings will have you healing
Never let them win you need to be in control
Because emotions can definitely take their toll

Her

So strong and aggressive it may seem
But all she wants is someone on her team
Blamed broken and battered
Her life is everything but shattered
Her emotions are something that is unknown
Instead they're represented in the actions shown.

She craves the intimacy and vulnerability
But being there for people is her ability
So sweet and nice and kind
But underneath is a very intelligent mind
Healing and peace is the destination
And getting there is her determination
I'm standing in awe that's for sure
Stand and clap for HER

Time Goes By

I hope that time goes by
And gives all the answers to what I ask why
I hope that all my wishes come true
And let's me be with the woman that is you
Never understood of what shall and can be
But I hope that you can stand tall by me
I want you to be free, beautiful as you can
But with you every day I grow into a man

Would've, Could've, Should've...

My mom always said
If they wanted to would
If they can they could
If they said they should
Don't make people a priority
When they treat you like an option
Mutual benefit is the base of the standard
If I talk, you talk. If you text me, I'll text you
But that will not be understood in today's youth

Self Care

No more toxic ways
No more sad days
No more waiting for a text
Today, tomorrow, the day after next
Saying yes to them but to yourself no
Will eventually make you explode
Love yourself, forget about the rest
Because you know you best
Take that trip
Catch a fish
Surround yourself around those that care
And forget about the ones that aren't there
If they wanted to they would
But don't you be a would've, could've, should
Do all the things you can
Because you are all you've got, man

Moving on

Sometimes they are there for a reason
Sometimes they are there for a season
Sometimes you leave for different views
Sometimes they leave for outgrowing you
One feels alone
The other doesn't care
One is home
The other is somewhere
Now is the time to focus on your self care
'Cause if it's true love they would be there

Mental Breakdown

What ifs are a bitch
What if she likes me
What if I move one more inch
What if I can't see
What if I fail miserably
What if I don't pass
What if I'm trash
Breathing hard my heart beating harder
Zoning out my vision becomes smaller
No one there
Makes you wonder if they care
Take care of your health
It's more important than wealth

Letting Things Happen

The ups are the best days of my life
Even the norms have their highlights
There are no bad ones maybe that's a sign
But the energy is so kind and benign
Knowing what could be is amazing
But also what could not is terrifying

So, the best is just enjoying the time spent
So you won't wonder where time went
What's meant to be will work out
There might be some doubt
If something is worth it be patient
Don't worry or question it
Know who you are. Live free, have fun
Because maybe the ride is only just begun

Wild Side

Mischievous as can be
Born in the wild almost seems
Behind the warm eyes and kind smile
Stands a man born to be wild
He drinks like a fish
While causes a ruckus in the midst
Drugs are no more a part of his life
But damn they made his body feel just right
Starting fights, chasing women, *woo weee!*
Man this guy knows how to make a scene
Self-destruct isn't the term for it
Because all the while he's confident
Only she can tame his ferocity
Her nature so strong and kind as can be
But…

She doesn't understand the wild man that's me

Black Love

So complicated to the foreign eye
The love that is shared is by a girl and guy
Some would question the methods, the sanity
Because solely this love is not shared by many

The pain and struggles when both get stuck
When she's down he lifts her up
When he reaches a door that he can't unlock
She's there to be his rock

Divided they are powerful from above
Combined they fly like a dove
That's the power of black love

What I Like

I like your big beautiful eyes
Somehow can light up the night sky
Your full luscious lips
Which I have been dying to kiss
I liiike the way you laugh
Or the way you walk into a room with class
I like your athleticism
You playing sports makes my body shiver
I like how you're so clean
Smelling like coco butter and looking pristine
Your curly hair is so cute
Playing with it will make me whhhhewwww
I like how you tease me and smile
That drives my body wild
Your touch so warm and gentle
I feel so safe and it's so sentimental
I like how your calm and never riled
It tames my inner wild
I like your body and its shape
Staring at you makes my heart race

Your voice strong but so soft
When we talk it's like my heart stopped
Your spirit is so strong
It's like a beautiful Brent Faiyaz song
Your love for family so unique
It makes my heart skip a beat
My feelings fly high like a kite
Because most of all it's you that I like

Sabotage

Sometimes it comes in waves
Every so often or maybe in a couple days
I fall for a soul someone pure as can be
Feelings arise and emotions unmistakably
But I'm worn and tattered
Hurt from the past all my relations battered
Instead of enjoying the ride and letting it sit
Out is my defense mode and I destroy it

It's not intentional, I don't mean it
I just want someone to fight for me and not quit
Deep down I feel like a monster from the past
So I ruin it so nothing further can amass
I don't want them to see the anger I possess
The destruction that causes such a mess

I'm changing and want for someone to see
But I can't hide from the monster that is me
I drink 'til alcohol touches my spleen
I'm not a nice person, I'm cruel and mean
I like to argue and fight
It's a release like an orgasm at night

I'm selfish, I hate people, I like the rain
Because the cold and wet helps numb the pain
The bad guy doesn't get the girl
He walks alone miserably in this cold world
If I don't get my way
I'll cut off an individual in a day
I can't have love, friends or an entourage
Because all I do is sabotage

Trust

Why can't I believe you?
Whatever you say I feel like it's not true
Your words sound so nice and sweet
But your actions are full of deceit
Filling up someone's head
With all the lies you spread
Now the moment has come true
Where I can't trust you

Doubt

Do you love her, do you love me?
Without reassurance there is no peace
One party is working, going all out
When the other doesn't, that leaves doubt
One person vibing and the feelings are strong
The other is nonchalant, leading you on

It's impossible to show my love to you
Because you remind me of a girl I knew
People say that they will be there
Some say they care
With her all I got was despair
I wonder at times do I wreck this?
Should I say fuck this trick?
Or leave my heart in her hands
And probably become a crippled man
DOUBT

www.ingramcontent.com/pod-product-compliance
Lightning Source LLC
Chambersburg PA
CBHW071223070526
44584CB00019B/3133